NOBODY IMPORTANT

Written by Lee J. Mavin

Illustrated by Karolina Piotrowska

Nobody Important
Copyright © 2023 by Lee J Mavin

All rights reserved. No part of this publication may be reproduced, distributed, or transmitted in any form or by any means, including photocopying, recording, or other electronic or mechanical methods, without the prior written permission of the author, except in the case of brief quotations embodied in critical reviews and certain other non-commercial uses permitted by copyright law.

Tellwell Talent
www.tellwell.ca

ISBN
978-0-2288-9315-8 (Hardcover)
978-0-2288-9314-1 (Paperback)

The Evil Ones attacked the Underlings with their savage swords and wicked ways. The once wise and creative world of the Underlings was undersiege with the enemies from the North.

They came with their fire and folly, mounting wild beasts
from above, raining down thunder and chaos
to the Western Lands of the Underlings.
They were lead by the Shouting King, a hairless monster
with a crown made from stolen Underling treasures.

The Underlings tried to respond, with a war of words from their elders but the Evil Ones seemed bent on destruction and tunneled further west.
The Underlings thought they could deter their might by broadcasting the terror to the world.

The Higher Elders and the Wise Chieftains chattered away,
devising plans to strike back
and the Artiest Artists painted their flags blood red
and cried to the world for help.

As the war grew and grew and the innocent Underlings
watched in horror. Their Northern lands were covered
in flame and terror and fear overcame them.
Most of the regular Underlings, went from confused to angry
and cried out for the war to end.

However one particular Underling by the name of **Nobody Important**, (Yes, that was his actual name!) came up with the most surprising and unrealistic plan to stop the war and bring peace to the world again.

Nobody Important was nothing special. He was overly average and exceptionly ordinary and was never really noticed until he changed the entire world forever.
He was the most famous Underling for being unknown and unheard of.
Until of course he stopped the war.

But how could such a strangely normal Underling cause such an unlikely impact, you ask?

Surely the Higher Elder Underlings and the Wise Chieftains would be the ones to bring peace with their cunning crafts, crashing over the Evil Ones.
They could sway their power with clever plans and rob the Evil Ones of their much needed fruits and grains.

Surely the Most Magic Illusionists of the Underling Order would be able to cast a spell over the war and make it all disappear and would be able to trick televise their vanishing to the new world.

Surely the Artiest Artists would save us all. They would paint such a horrid picture of what these Evil Ones have created, that when everyone sees it, the Evil Ones would cower and cry and return to their dark dungeons.

But no, the Higher Elder Underlings and the Wise Chieftains only made the Evil Ones more ferocious that their hungry warriors struck them with might and they tore through their farms, stuffing their mouths with their berries and wheat.

The Most Magic Illusionists failed too, angering the Evil Ones
with their not so terrifying, televised spells.
The Evil Ones quickly mimiced their spells and televised
their own lies to their people and their armies
grew and grew with blind soldiers.

And even the Artiest of Artists could not save us,
as the Evil Ones spawned their own painters and sculpters
in faraway darkness. They erected statutes of their masters
and painted magnificent murials of their conquests,
as more of their people grew to believe their plight.

So our last hope, was Nobody Important. He was just
an uncomplicated Underling that nobody
really knew too well.

How could someone so unfamiliar
bring a stop to all this madness?

Well, Nobody Important, was a bit of a poet,
so I guess he wasn't nobody important after all.
He could also sing his words with such sweetness,
even the darkest tombs in the far reaches of the Evil
Dungeons, were lit when he spoke.

He appeared in front of all the Evil Ones and the entire army held up their swords and listened.

He sang:

All of you sword-wielders

You boulder tossing

War mongers

You have created monstrous mechanisms

That crush the earth and drain its life

Then the Underlings circled around behind him. The Higher Elders and the Wise Chieftains put down their parchments and the Most Magic Illustionists lowered their wands. The Artiest Artists crawled in next to him and put down their paint brushes.

Nobody Important continued:

All of you wiser word sayers

You trick twisting

Peace criers

You have fed the monsters with your own fears

And now you mirror each other lives

The Underlings looked at the Evil Ones and suddenly they didn't seem so different.

And that was all it took. A look at each other, face to face, after hearing those words sang by Nobody Important. The war ended quickly and peace was finally restored to the lands.

The Underlings went on with all their Underlinging business and the Evil Ones became less evil.

Nobody Important went back to his overly average
and exceptionly ordinary life.

His face was soon forgotten
but his words were forever remembered.

The young Underlings and infant (not so) Evil Ones often sing
his words as the sun sets over the Western peaks.
Their sweet song echoes into the far North
and trickles down into the West.

War mongers

You have created monstrous mechanisms

That crush the earth and drain its life

Peace criers

You have fed the monsters with your own fears

And now you mirror each other's lives

www.ingramcontent.com/pod-product-compliance
Lightning Source LLC
LaVergne TN
LVHW071651060526
838200LV00029B/424